One Minute Movies

Chuck Warren

Enjoy!

2/18/08

Inquiries should be addressed to:

Chuck Warren

PO Box 1612

Holland, MI 49422

Info.pendragon@gmail.com

www.thependragon.com

Tightrope Publishing

ISBN - 978-0-6151-7816-5

ISBN 978-0-6151-7816-5

51495 >

9 780615 178165

For ACCLDJ,
and OOBTKBSJJW,
and 100 others who've influenced
who I was, and who I am now.

Please support your local animal shelter,
and please consider adopting one of the
wonderful pets in need instead of purchasing.

Thanks to Michael Shead for the back cover photo.

To me, a movie is so much more that just a story in pictures. It's an experience, where the colors, the background, and the interaction between the characters all come together to transport me from here and now to there and then. That's what I tried to give you on these pages, some little screenplays, which are meant not just to be read, but visualized and felt. These "one minute movies" are mixed in with the poetry.

As you read, try to imagine the scene playing out before you, see the splash of color or light, and feel the love, pain, or triumph that at first looks two dimensional laying there in front of you. Let yourself become one of the people in the scene, and just for a moment, take a break from the here and now.

Contents

Introduction

Hello.....

My name is Chuck, and since they say that admitting the problem is the first step towards recovery, I guess I'm going to come right out and say it. I, well, I am.......a writer.

I started writing when I was about 13, I remember my first time like it was yesterday. It was only a paragraph, not much really, but I still remember the way it made me feel. If I had known more about it, I would have recognized that I had a problem, even then.

I considered myself a social writer for years, only writing a page or two once or twice a week. Usually I would write after dinner or early evening, just enough to wind down after a hard day, or help me sleep. I didn't think I really needed to write back then, it was just fun. I knew a lot of other people who were doing it.

After a while, I started to write more and more, poems and paragraphs weren't enough anymore. I needed to write several pages before I felt that familiar rush, only it didn't last as long either. No sooner would I put away the pen and paper than I would feel that pull again. Sometimes I would stay up all night, writing alone with just a desk lamp to light the pages. Even then, I kept telling myself I could quit at any time.

As the years went by, my habit became more and more of a problem. I began to leave for work late, trying to get down that one last word before I went out the door. I was writing on anything I could find, matchbook covers, napkins, even scraps of paper. I would use anything I could to tide me over until I could get home to my desk.

Lately, I have come to realize the cost of my problem. I have three computers, a laptop, a palm pilot, and at least a dozen notepads. I can't walk past a newsstand or convenience store without stopping to look at the pens and pencils. I keep telling myself, just one more, maybe a Bic Widebody, or a Pilot Easytouch this time, and then I'll give it up. But, I keep going back, I keep picking up another ream of paper. These days, things have gotten so bad I sometimes wake up to find several empty pages laying around me on which I tried write something in the middle of the night, only I don't remember ever picking up the pen.

(cont)

(cont)

    So here, on these pages, I hope to pour out my soul, and put my problem out there for all to see. I have even joined a group where we meet once a week to share our stories about this terrible affliction. I hope that maybe, just maybe, we can band together and save each other from this fate. Together, we can learn to look each other in the eye and say without shame, I admit it, I can't help it, I am a writer.

Chuck Warren

November 1, 2007

One Minute Movies

There's this movie
Well, more than one really,
They all keep playing
Over and over in my head.
Wishes, like a candle in a drafty room,
One window open to let in hope,
The firelight flickers against the wall,
But the breeze threatens
To snuff out the flame.
Regrets, like an old war wound
That won't heal no matter how
We medicate, recuperate,
They always need stitches
To keep them closed.
Memories, like a hawk on the wind
Soaring to heights far out of view,
Then skimming past my ear
And brushing me with a wingtip
So I don't ever lose sight.
And love,
Present, past,
And future tense,

(cont)

(cont)

Love settles in a rocking chair
With an open book and fuzzy slippers,
Occasionally peering at me
Over the top of the glasses
That have slipped down her nose,
And smiles.
Short films, glimpses,
Of an everyday life,
One minute movies
And the audience is me.

Too Hard Love

It's just too hard,
This love stuff,
I think to myself
As we fail to see
Eye to eye again.
It's just too hard,
I think, until
She touches me,
Caressing my face
With the back
Of her hand.
And I think,
It's just too easy
This love stuff,
Just too easy,
As she smiles.

Objects

I closed the cabinet door
And I stared at me
Staring back at me
Raised a hand
To touch my face
And I could see the scars
On the back of my hand
On my forehead
Just left of my lip
And deep in my eyes
I could see the scars
On my heart
And on my soul
As clear as day
For as anyone can tell you
Objects in the mirror
Are always
Closer
Than they appear

Dot

Let me see her
before her time comes
let me see her
and say goodnight

let me see her
before her journey
let me tell her
she'll walk in light

give her peace
and give her pleasure
give her all
she missed in life

take away
her pain and burdens
take away
the strain and strife

a rite of passage
a fine procession
give her horses
on which to ride

(cont)

(cont)

let her see
the ones she loved
waiting there to
stand by her side

Lord let me see her
before the times gone
let me hold
her hand once more

let her know
that love awaits
then show her through
the open door

For Dorothy Warren

Song

I can hear it playing
In the back of my mind
Like a freight train
Running hard in the distance
I can faintly hear that soft refrain
The simple notes that hide
The jagged edges and
Sharpened spikes of the music
So many years go by
In a blink and a whisper
And then at once
The days are gone
And the time has come
To pay the man
The one who carries the horn
To hear the sound it makes
To hear him play
That tune for you
That song you heard play
In the back of your mind
On a warm sunny day
When a chill runs down
Your spine as if a shadow
Had just passed across
The un-turned ground

(cont)

(cont)

Where you would lie someday
Where people will stand
Holding each others hand
And softly hum that melody
That same simple tune
Just out of key but clear
Still clear enough
And you will still hear it
It will not stop for you
It will play on and on

Speak

Speak, I said,
Come on Kodi, speak,
Come on boy...

He cocked his head
from side to side,
Staring at me intently
with his brow furrowed
Before finally he said
What exactly
would you like me to say,
And, are you really sure
that's what you want?

I'm always in the room,
I've hear all of your calls,
see everything you do
day in and day out.
You know that old saying,
If walls could talk?
Well they got it wrong.

Just think for a minute,
Do you know how much
you say out loud,
how often you talk to me
thinking I don't understand?

(cont)

I've got your PIN numbers,
Your social security number,
I even know the password
For all of your accounts.
And by the way,
the doorknob thing?
Complete myth.
We all know how it works.

I sat in shock
For a full five minutes,
Then composed myself.

Bark, I said,
Come on Kodi, bark,
Come on boy…

Yeah, he said,
That's what I thought.
Now lets discuss
The treat situation,
I believe there may be
Some discrepancies there.

grace

i
looked
behind me
and i
saw me
walking back
the other way
and i thought
to myself
as i faded
away
there but for
the grace
of God
go
i

climate control

sixty
or sixty one
sixty four
or sixty five
but not
sixty three
never sixty three
seventy
no not seventy
sixty six
sometimes
yes sixty six
but not today
sixty
or sixty one
maybe, yes,
sixty one

Cards

Don't slam the door
he said, throwing his hand
out to stop her from
doing just that.
What are you doing?
she asked, squinting
as if she couldn't
make out the details
in the brightly lit room
Building a house of cards
he replied, hunched over
the dark brown coffee table.
The breeze from the door
might knock it down.
See how they lay against
each other, balanced
so they won't fall, and
how together they hold up
the next level
so it can continue to grow.
I've been working on it
all morning, he said,
which was obvious since
he was still in his PJ's.

(cont)

(cont)

As he lifted his hand
to start a new level,
she sighed,
and shook her head.
It's kind of stuffy in here,
She said, as she
walked over to open
the sliding glass door.

Framed

I walk, I run
I eat and sleep,
And I watch
And remember
The things that
I can
Each memory
A picture
A snapshot
I've taken
To keep for myself
Or to share
With other people
I pick up a frame
Reach through,
And grab hold
Of landscape
Or linen
Of satin or steel
And I pull back the image
Till it fits in the borders
Set it carefully on the mantle
To look at once in a while

(cont)

(cont)

But there's more to the picture
Each one hides some of the story
Outside of the margins
Trimmed off of the canvas
I, and you, only see the image
Selected, edited, trimmed down to fit
Protected by glass
And placed in the frame

Dawn

There's that moment in time
Each morning, in the early hours,
When I lay in bed not awake
And yet not asleep.
The white down comforter,
(What a perfect name)
Wrapped tight around me,
The pillow cushions my head,
I'm protected from monsters
Both real and imagined.
I can feel her body pressed
Against my back, one arm
Draped across my chest.
Her warmth is my warmth,
Her breath is a feather
Lightly teasing my skin.
In these moments,
When the sunlight is still
A soft glow searching
For a way around
The window shades,
And the shadows soften
As they slowly retreat,
In these moments
There's no doubt
That Heaven exists.

Ridin'

It's such a long way
So far to go
And damn that sun
The pavement burns
My tired feet
Only half the way
And can't go back
Look at all them
Ridin' in their fancy cars
Radio loud,
Air turned up
So cold I can see
Their breath making
Patches of fog
Against the crystal
Clear windshields
We're all just
Walkin' around dyin'
Anyway
Might as well
Try hitchin' a ride
So far to walk
Hold out your thumb
Can't hurt to try
We might as well
Be ridin' too,
Might just as well
Be ridin'.

If

What if, she asked,
we never met?
what if we were never
meant to be?
I thought
for a moment,
then I looked at the sky.
I always look there
for answers.
What if, I answered,
what if dogs could talk,
and rain fell up
from the ground,
I replied.
She looked at me
like I was slipping
in my old age,
I'm being serious
she said, and I knew
that she was.
I smiled, and I said,
If we never met,
then I would
be somewhere else
right now, alone,

(cont)

(cont)

looking up at the stars
and dreaming aloud,
a hint of sadness
would show on my face.
What if, I would say,
what if I never meet her?
What if we are never
meant to be?

Duck

I noticed a lot
more white hair lately
I said,
as she plopped
next to me
on the couch
to watch some TV.
She looked at me closely,
then reached out and
plucked one violently
from my beard.
You know,
she replied,
I think you're right.
Maybe it's stress,
she joked.
I thought for a moment
and then I said,
funny you should
mention that.
I noticed that there
is more white on the
right side of my face
than the left.
She wanted to know
why I thought that
was stress-related.

(cont)

(cont)

Because, I replied
with a grin,
whenever we're
in the car,
or on the couch,
you are always on
my right hand side.
One of these days
I really should learn
to duck.

Hurt

The pain was too intense
Too much for anyone to bear
Cutting like a thousand knives
Rusty and ragged, tearing at my flesh
And the blood poured out like water
Weak and thin, running like rain
To seep away in to the earth
Bitter food for another crop
And I prayed
For the salvation of life
And I begged
For the deliverance of death
But the healing wouldn't come
couldn't come from me
no matter how I cried
no matter who, or how I asked
I wished for drought to parch my throat
And dull my senses
I wanted for strength
To stand alone and turn away
And I prayed
For the sanctity of life
And I begged
For the sanity of death
But the sunrise of another day
Was always there to greet me

(cont)

(cont)

My eyes aflame in the early dawn
Too tired to get to my feet
Too sore to stay prone
I died a little more each day
Until the light began to burn my skin
like fire licking at my soul
And I prayed
For another chance at life
And I begged
To be overlooked by death
Battered and bandaged
With blood dried on my lips
I crawled into the light of day
To lap at the clear waters
That ran outside my open door
And feast on the fruit
That grew from the trees
And I healed, and I stood again
And I wept
At the precious gift of life
And I smiled
At the hollow face of death

9.1

hot today, at least ninety-six
third day in a row
close to triple digits.
a sticky, blanketing heat,
shirt hangs from my back
like laundry too soon
off the back yard line.
but there's something else
hiding near the sunrise that's
beginning to blind me
on my morning drive.
there's a gray tint fading
the summers bright
yellows and greens,
a sharp edge to the morning
greets me on the
other side of the door.
i'm not ready, no, wait,
i reluctantly sigh
and take that back.
the colors of fall, the silence
of winter, one years
end means another begins.
new promise, new purpose,
resolutions and rebirth.

(cont)

(cont)

soon nineties will give way
to sixties, then fifties,
and the edge will cut
a little deeper, the gray
a little darker, and in
the early morning chill
i will wish for today.

Catch This

Driving back from
out of state, I was
greeted by
a sign at the border
that said,
"Welcome to Michigan"
underneath it said,
"Great Lakes, Great Times".
So I got to thinking,
(which happens a lot)
it seems like everywhere
I look, I'm hit with some
catchy phrase
or slogan. So.
I decided I should
have my own,
a little phrase that
identifies some unique
quality or ability
of mine, something
people will
remember me by.
So, from now on,
I will introduce myself as
"Chuck Warren"
"Great typing, Great spelling".

(cont)

(Cont)

Or maybe
"Chuck Warren"
"Not too tall, but nice beard".
Or even,
"Chuck Warren"
"Not even spiders scare me".
I might need to work
on that, a little,
and you should too.
Get your own,
I see a trend forming here.

It's OK

It's okay, you go on home
I'll be alright here
At least for a while
Thank you for leading
And lighting the way
But I know that you're tired
So you go on ahead

It's okay, let go of my hand
I can find my way
For the rest of the trip
Thanks for picking me up
Whenever I fell
But I know that it's time
I take care of myself

It's okay, you don't have to look back
There's no unfinished task
Nothing here to regret
I can close up the shop
And sweep out the dust
I'll make sure that you're proud
Of what I leave behind

It's okay, you can turn off the light
I'll be able to see
Where you walked on the path
I'll just follow the footsteps
That you've made in the sand
And I know I'll be safe
Till I come to the end

It's okay, you walk on home
I'll just be a few minutes
Then I'll be along too
Find a place in the sun
Sit and rest for a while
And don't worry about me
I'll be along pretty soon.

Shades

In a flash I saw the universe for what it was
And in the same instant I understood.
I saw it in all of its glory, spectacular, naked,
Not the planets and stars, or clouds of gas,
Not the structure and order of the cosmos,
But the light and color that were its soul.
I saw the reflections, the spectrum of light
Bounced back from every single thing,
Piercing my eyes and burning a hole
Into the deepest recesses of my mind.
The reds appeared as hot as fire,
Like molten rock I saw it flow
From one thing to another,
Gently caressing everything it touched.
The greens as soft as new mown grass,
Had a voice that sang of early spring
and texture I longed to feel deep within.
The color purple, strong and majestic,
Beckoned me to let my fingers
Sink deep beneath the velvet surface.
And the black whispered of the unknown,
Hinting at everything, and nothing, all at once.
But the blue, the blue stayed calm and silent,
Ebbing and flowing among the heavens,
Sometimes becoming a shade deeper
Or brighter if it felt the need arise.

(cont)

(cont)

And I watched the light dance from one end
Of the universe to the other, until I turned
And I noticed the grays, still, like shadows,
out near the edges where nothing moved.
And I knew, that's where the sadness lived,
I watched for life, a glint of light, and then
I turned back and searched out the blue.

choice

we make
conscious decisions
you and i
we make decisions
everyday
to live or die
i choose the path
i walk
i choose to remain
alive
but I would
give it all
i would walk away
from everything
i have
to help you
to make the choice
to make the change
to find some kind
of peace, because
the choices you make
and choices you don't
are the ones
you have to
live, or die
with everyday
i know because
at last i finally
made a choice

Aud's Wish

To the sea
Release my soul
Unto the sea
That I may roam
On wind and water
Will I dance
The restless waves
Will bear me home

To the air
Release my soul
Into the air
That I may fly
Upon the wind
I'll soar aloft
The seagulls wings
Will lift me high

Into the sun
Release my soul
Release me to
The sky above
But keep me close
Within your heart
It's there I will
Live on in love

Landscape

I walked miles, across hills and valleys, deserts and mountains, to find myself at the front of a huge black house. I sat on the ground with my head against the door, waiting for someone to let me in. Every day I would reach up to try the handle, to see if it was unlocked or someone had noticed me there, but day after day it remained closed.

So I sat, and I waited. Weeks, then months went by, but parched and withered I waited still. With my back to the door the landscape panned out in front of me, charred and barren, blackened earth stretched as far as I could see. No sound, no movement, even the air was still as death. In time I grew comforted by the emptiness, there were no surprises, no problems to solve or failures to face, no sadness, no love, just the coal black ground reaching out in to the distance.

Then one day I saw it, a glimpse of color, just a flash so quick I tried to dismiss it. But it was there, and I watched that spot until I could take it no longer, and finally I forced myself up from the ground. And I began to walk, shaky at first, unsure of each step, and every bone in my body crying out for me to return to the door, and rest again in the shadows of the huge black house I'd known for so long. But the color beckoned me until I could no longer ignore it, and I set out to see what I would find.

After two days I approached the spot to find a beautiful flower, one like I had never seen before. I stood in awe, drinking in the blues and purples of the petals, and the vivid greens of the flowers stem, until I ached to feel the softness of it against my skin. But my hands were black from the barren earth and I was afraid to spoil the beauty before me. I wiped my hands against my clothes, and to my surprise the dust fell away as if it had never been there at all, and as I gently touched the leaves and petals, I felt something I had forgotten existed, I felt joy.

As I stood again I caught another glimpse of color further away in the distance, further out across the barren landscape. I took one step towards it and then stopped, turning back to the house just in time to see a black robed, faceless figure close the door I had been leaning against for so long. I hesitated, but only for a second, before I turned again and took a step, and then I slowly started to walk.

Paradox

I turned in time
to see
a single tear
trace its way
slowly,
gently,
down her face.
Why are you
crying?
I asked her.
Love
She replied,
and began
to laugh.
I don't
understand
I said to her,
are you crying
because
you're happy
or sad?
Both she replied
with a sigh.
Love she said,
with a smile
and a tear,
a desperate dream
an infinite odyssey,
such a perfect paradox.

sharp

goddam edge.
goddam the edge.
i can't stay here,
i can't balance very long.
it's too hard sometimes,
too hard to walk this line,
to place one foot
directly in front of the other.
anything else and i'm over.
anything less and i'll fall.
maybe that wouldn't be so bad,
at least it would be easier.
wouldn't have to pay attention
anymore, wouldn't have
to watch my step.
wouldn't wear out
all my shoes
walking that fine thin line,
walking that rusted razor,
walking along
that goddam edge.

Bela (beagle eye view)

Food, food, food
food, food? Food,
food. Maybe here,
food, food, no, here?
Food, food, food,
food. How about
here, food,
food, food, food,
food, food.
Wait, wait, no,
Ok. Food, food,
food, food?
FOOOOD!!!!
YEAH, FOOD!
Ok, nap.

Ok, food, food,
Food, food? Food,
food, food,
maybe here, food,
no? Ok, how about
here, food, food,
food....

Tides

The beach is the only place
A man can feel
His is the only
Soul that's real
or something like that
The opening verse to
an old Who song
plays through my head
it's from Quadrophenia
I think, or Tommy
maybe.
sitting here, staring out
over the sand and sea,
the surf surges forward
just to relinquish
its claim on the land
again and again
as if playfully reminding us
she can take it all back
any time she pleases.
the sound pulsing in my ears
drowns out the ringing
of phones, the beeping
of machines, the traffic
of the highway and city streets

(cont)

(cont)

Bellboy, I remember,
is the name of the song,
as alone I sit and listen
to the sea
she softly sighs
the water her voice
the waves are her accent
the tide is her mood
changing at only her will
not mine, not ours
over and over
she speaks her peace
hoping, maybe
someday we'll listen
someday
maybe
someone will hear

Half-inch, Split-second

One half inch nearly caused my demise that day in March, as I ran along the dock at the edge of the lagoon, I raised my foot about a half an inch less than I should have, and caught the toe of my sneaker in the hose that lay coiled like a snake in my path.

The man three houses down was doing the dishes and watching through the kitchen window when he saw me fly out on to the early spring ice that covered the lagoon. It happened so fast that I never even tried to catch myself as I went through the opaque sheet covering the frigid water, and settled underneath the overhanging dock. If the dishwashing man had blinked he never would have seen it happen.

The water was so cold that I stood like a statue on the bottom in complete shock. I would have remained there, weighed down by my winter clothing if the hood of my parka hadn't floated just high enough above my head to create a handle for the neighbor's groping hand to catch. He hauled my limp body back up to the surface before my own family ever knew what had happened. I coughed and sputtered as I lay there in the cold mud until finally I spit up the one split-second that had separated me from eternity in the form of a watery grave.

I was eight years old and far too young for a parent to bury. I lived in fear of the water for years after that, and didn't learn to swim until I was thirteen. One half-inch, one split-second. Not much in the grand scheme of things when you think about it.

Box

what do you have
in your hands he said,
as she held out
an ornate silver platter
with a simple oak box
placed carefully
in the center.
my heart she replied
handing everything
carefully
over to him.
he took the platter
and the box and
placed them both
upon the table
and then pressed his ear
against the wooden lid.
it was soft, but steady
and clearly
he could hear the beat
as her precious gift
counted the seconds
and the days
that her love was his
to claim for his own.

Dog Day

Too much to do today,
you have to get up!
I'd let myself out,
but I still need you
to believe we can't
work the doorknob.
At least until
the signal comes
and we take over.
Come on, come on,
I can see the sky
is beginning to
get light, I gotta
get going before
Jake the Black Lab
from next door
gets all the good smells.
Where's my checklist,
Oh here it is.
Let's see, I need to
roll in something,
bark at that squirrel
that always sits
one branch too high,
then there's still
lots to eat out there
around the yard.

(cont)

(cont)

Come on already,
it's not that cold out,
that's what these pads
are for, oh,
you don't have them.
Well, then hurry up
with the artificial ones
already, time's a wastin',
there's so much to do.

Sanctuary

Hollow, hurting,
my lungs burn
and my head pounds
from breathing the dust
that settles in my wake
The blood on my hands
looks pale, washed clean,
faded in the filtered light
from the stained glass window
above my head.
Can anyone see me?
I ask myself,
can anyone look
down upon me,
and believe,
what's done is done
and what's to be will be.
In a moment of clarity
I see myself,
Alone and standing,
my arms outstretched
my head thrown back,
I cry out, and the silence shatters
falling heavily to the ground.

(cont)

(cont)

Bending, I collect the shards
careful not to cut myself,
no fresh wounds, I tell no one,
I will bleed no more I say aloud.
I place the pieces
on the dusty shelf,
then turn away to leave.
Pulling my coat
along with my courage,
tight around me
against the biting wind
I carefully retrace my steps
back the way I came,
back out through
the open door.

Steam

I never saw it coming,
the image that confronted me
in the mirror one morning
late last march.
I wasn't prepared, although
I suppose I could have been.
It's not like it should have been
much of a surprise, but somehow
it caught me off guard.
I wiped the steam from the mirror
and there, staring back at me,
was someone I'd never seen before.
He had shorter hair than me,
He was wearing
A button-down shirt and slacks.
Slacks.
I would never wear slacks,
I'm a jeans kind guy.
And the glasses
perched above his nose
looked as strange as
the large patch of white hair
that was sprinkled through his beard.
Neatly trimmed beard at that.
I stared at him for a long time,
wondering how he got there.

(cont)

(cont)

How did this man come to replace
the boy with the grease stains on his hands,
the carefree kid with the gold hoop earring,
the young man with long blond hair.
How did this man take the place
of the face I once saw every morning,
framed by the steam in the bathroom mirror.
The face I still expect to see.

Shark attack, Swab.

So, how did you get the cast she asked.

Well, I said, after a day of diving
off the Florida coast,
I was back in the boat
packing up my gear when
I heard a shout from the water,
and looked just in time to see
a large Great White Shark circling
a couple who had yet to get out.

She gasped, staring at my
blue fiberglass covered arm
what did you do she said.

Now, I've had some experience
with Great Whites I answered,
so I dove back in the water
with my razor sharp knife and swam
between the man-eating shark and his prey

She gasped again,
waiting for me to continue.

I had the knife in my teeth
when suddenly the shark turned on me.

(cont)

In seconds he was on me,
And locked down on my arm
forcing me to pull the knife
with my left hand,
and jab him in the nose.

Did he swim away she asked

Yes, but he came back
for one more pass, so I
kicked him in the gills and
we all scrambled back aboard the boat.
Wow, she said, that's amazing,
you saved those people
for sure!

I smiled, and picked up
the grocery bags with
my left hand, and headed
for the door. As I walked away
I looked back and smiled
and figured I'd better
set things straight.

Actually, I said
with a twinkle in my eye
as the door began to
hiss slowly shut, it was dark
and I just tripped over the dog.

mud

i know that road
i know it well
even though
i have chosen
not to walk it anymore
i can still see it there
off to my left
it runs parallel
to the one
i travel now
and i see you there
i can see how easily
the mud
from the pock-marked
and uneven surface
splashes up on your clothes
and streaks your face
i can see the tracks
your tears have left
as they washed down
your cheeks
to dry in the dirt
i can see how
the sludge and debris
from the road you walk
comes off your hands

(cont)

(cont)

when you touch
those around you
and loosens your grip
on all you try
so hard to hold
i know that road
i can see you there
across the field
just off to my left
and i wish you would
just turn your head
so you'd see me wave
and hear that i'm calling
it's not easy but still i know
you can make it
across to this side
where it's safe to walk
where the way is well lit
just turn your head
and you'll see i'm here
take a few steps
off that hard-traveled road
just hold out your hand
and i'll guide you across

Relativity

There were bags by the door
When I came home.
Not just bags, but luggage.
Her luggage.
She was sitting in the kitchen,
Quietly in the dark.
Don't turn on the light
She said,
I don't want to see your face.
You're leaving I said.
Why? I thought we were happy.
She sighed.
The light from a streetlamp
Was enough to see her
When she reached for my hand.
I have to go she said.
I have things to do.
I knew there was nothing
I could say,
In the back of my mind
I had known for years
That one day she would fly.
She smiled sadly
And let go of my hand.
I'm sorry she said,
It's a matter of perspective.
I can see that no matter

(cont)

(cont)

What we do, where we go,
One thing will never change.
Everything
And everyone
Is moving in relation
To something,
Or someone,
else.

Pages

I pulled a book
down from the dusty shelf
where it had rested
For so many years
and sat down
in my favorite chair.
With a hint of excitement
I began a journey,
I took my first step
As I opened the cover
To page number one.
When I reached page fifteen
I had become smitten
With a princess from afar
By one hundred I had sailed
To the Spice Islands,
Seychelles and Azores
Through two-fifty I fought pirates,
And explored foreign lands,
Africa, Asia, all fell away
Behind me as I reached
Four hundred and beyond.
I felt pain and joy
Love and lust,
And the people at my side
Were my friends to the end.

(cont)

(cont)

Some died or were killed,
And some married
And found peace,
And I loved them all, like family
As I journeyed across
The thin paper universe
With it's worn leather boundaries.
I came away with scars
And wealth, as I won or lost
A battle, a bet, or a bargain
With the turn of each page.
As I turned the last page,
Wishing for more, I felt
A loss, an emptiness
Left by the people and places
I was leaving behind.
Gently I placed the book
Back in it's resting place,
I hesitated at the door
Before a flick of the switch
Plunged my adventures,
And some of my dreams,
Back into the darkness,
Where they waited once again
On the dusty shelf.

Colors

Blue
she pours me
out like water
I pool there
all around
her feet

Gold
she sings me
like a sonnet
I float upon
on the
gentle breeze

Green
she grows me
like a garden
I stand tall
like the
summer wheat

White
she speaks me
like the wind
I drift
across
the calmest seas

(cont)

(cont)

Red
she loves me
like a fire
within
her flame
my passion burns

Black
she writes me
as a story
on empty
pages
I await

Grey
she leaves me
overcast
I wait
until
.the sun returns

All
she gives me
in her colors
I'm brought
to life
as she creates

Time to Go

We sit upon
a hard wooden bench
watching the patterns
in the surface
of the stream as it
slowly trickles past.
And the silence
is palpable, tangible,
until I hear it
shatter like glass
when she finally speaks,
and she speaks
in no more than a whisper
when she says to me
it's time to go now,
time to go.
And she takes
my hand in hers,
as we walk with our backs
to the setting sun
across the velvet field.
bright green grass
like water flows
in all directions.
We hover on the surface,
no sound comes from
beneath our feet,

(cont)

(cont)

and I hear her voice
ring in my head.
as her wing tip
brushes softly
against my shoulder.
She says to me
once more,
it's time to go now,
then she leads
me gently along
for the rest of the journey,
she shows me the way
as we walk back home.

Coffee

This is getting weirder by the minute I said. I swear, I was just dreaming that I was dreaming.

John looked at me and smiled. You are dreaming he said.

I stared at him for a full minute. If I'm dreaming, how is it that I know I'm dreaming? I asked him

Ah, he said, if you know you're dreaming, then why don't you wake up?

I leaned back in my chair to think about that for a minute. How do I know I'm not really awake, and you're dreaming? I said.

John laughed. Listen to me, he said. What were you dreaming before you woke up just now?

I thought for a minute, I was dreaming that I was dreaming. How can that be? I asked. It seemed so real.

And this? John asked, spreading his arms to indicate the room, doesn't this seem real?

Ok, I said, if this is actually a dream, then why do I taste this coffee?

I picked up the cup and put it to my lips, but there was nothing in it. I slowly turned the cup over and set it back on the saucer.

What coffee? John asked me? I motioned towards the table, but the cup was gone. Man, I said, this is weird. But, the dream I had a few minutes ago was….. so…. real….

I was fuzzy again, my thoughts not quite formed. Someone was calling me…wake up I heard, it was Mary's voice. Wake up, you're dreaming she said.

I came fully awake as I sat up. I stared around the room, trying to get my bearings again. Mary was sitting in the chair by the fire, staring at me. What is it? She asked.

Man, I said, this is getting weirder by the minute I said. I was just dreaming that I was dreaming. I reached for the coffee cup on the table.

i swear

i can save me
i don't need your help.
i can do it any time,
whenever i get
good and ready
thank you.

i can save me
probably tomorrow
or maybe the day after
just need to
prepare a little
get some stuff together
then i'll be just fine

i can save me
it won't be the first time
but this is the last
i mean it this time
i won't go back again
no matter what, i swear
you'll see.

i can save me
please don't you help
i don't want it, don't need it
just leave me be
please, i can

save me

Shooting Star

She'd brought his coat home,
and she hung it on the rack by the door,
right where he'd placed it every night
for the last six years.
Still, not a tear showed in her eyes,
not a trickle of sorrow
graced her pretty face.
We sat in the uncomfortable silence
until she finally spoke,
answering a question I'd asked
nearly an hour before.
"Yeah, of course I miss him" she said,
"I'll miss him every day."
I stared out the window
at the cardinal perched on the feeder,
a splash of blood against the pure white
of the snow covered evergreens.
"I wish I could have done something" I said,
I couldn't think of anything more profound.
"I wish I could have slowed him down."
She smiled at me, and I felt as if
she knew something the rest of us did not.
"He was a shooting star," she said.
"He was too fast for us to catch".
I couldn't think of a better way
to say what I had been thinking.

(cont)

(cont)

He was too fast, and he went too far,
and he left us all behind.
I nodded my head, and looked back to the window
but I couldn't let go of one single thought.
After a while she brought me some tea,
and I held the cup to warm my hands.
"Yes, he was a shooting star,
but excess isn't success." I quietly said.
She stared at me, and then started to cry,
and cradled her face in her hands.
I heard her whisper to herself
"He lived himself to death."

Home To You (a song?)

I set the sails and then
I stepped back to the wheel
I felt the breeze against my back
I felt the waves against the keel
A quarter turn to port
I checked my course against
The setting sun
And asked the wind
To blow me back to you

I pulled the anchor back
On board and stowed my gear
I checked the tides upon the chart
And asked the stars which way to steer
I left my fears upon the beach
And washed my troubles from
My weathered hands
And asked the sea to bring
Me back to you

I left my prints in the sands
Of some far off lands
But they're erased by the tides and the foam
And now the seagulls cry
Show the way as they fly
And I know it's time once again to go home

(cont)

(cont)

The moonlight shining on
The water shows the way
Through lonely days and endless nights
I followed far across the waves
A glimpse of light on the horizon
You're my shelter from
The raging storm
I begged the sea to bring
Me back to you

Take the Wheel

The road blurs slightly
As the ride goes on
The trees fly by
Before the setting sun
I lean back heavy
In my seat and sigh
Take the wheel Babe
I'm just too tired to drive

The day fades slowly
As we count the miles
The lights come on
Behind the dashboard dials
The white line swims
Before my aching eyes
Take the wheel Babe,
I'm just too tired to drive

Another day
Another roadside station
Another night
Another destination
We keep on pushing
Harder all the while
Please take the wheel Babe
I'm far too tired to drive

(cont)   67

(cont)

No matter where we head
No matter which direction
Whichever way we turn
At every intersection
I know we'll always make it
We'll get home alive
I know you'll take the wheel Babe
When I'm too tired to drive

Journey

Standing, waiting,
For the same train
I'd ridden
The day before
And the day before that
I saw an old man
walking along
the edge of the road.
He was moving
quickly, and steadily,
using a tree branch
as his walking stick.
His shoes were worn,
his beard unkempt,
and a smile creased
his deeply tanned
and wrinkled face.
How long have you
been walking
I asked him, when he
stopped beside me,
and where are you going?
He turned to face me,
and slowly shook his head.
I can't remember,
but I know that I
am making
very good time,

(cont)

(cont)

he replied looking
at his empty wrist
where a watch may
have once rested.
How will you know
when you've
reached the end?
I asked him, puzzled.
I'll know, he said,
but it's not today,
I've still got quite
a long way to go.
He brushed the dust
off his arms and legs,
creating a little cloud
around him, like an
aura, or a halo
and then he said,
I must be on my way.
He waved to me as
he picked up the pace,
and then called out
before he disappeared
there's so much left
for me to do and
I've only just begun,
He said,
my journey's
only just begun.

smoke

again, i saw her
floating just
above my head,
a vision,
white wisps
of smoke,
beautiful, elusive.
i wanted to
reach up
to touch, to know,
but i was afraid
she would
dissipate,
scattered
by my hand
like the ashes
of some distant
memory.
so instead
i watched,
i wished,
and i waited
until at last
she flew off

(cont)

(cont)

to her palace
in the night sky,
leaving me
behind to dream,
of silver,
of sable,
and of castles
in the clouds.

One Red Rose

Pale white sky
Dark stone bridge
Grey steel rails
Gusting winds
Dampened coats
Knotted belts
Crumbling curb
Paper cup
Pot-holed street
Tire tracks
Silver pool
One red rose

step back

step away man,
just step away
put it down
take one step back
you don't need it
you don't even
want it
anymore
i know
i should know
just step away
let it fall there
in the dust
beneath you
where it belongs
beneath you
out of the way
and take one
step back
just let it go
and step away

9.11

They took the twins
down in a flash,
a cloud of dust
that blocked the light
from freedom's torch
for just a moment,
and in a moment,
changed the course
of history, for one
and for us all.

They took the twins
down like castles,
sand in the path
of the rising tide.
A tide of hate,
of intolerance,
water rising against
the fragile levee
sheltering the
eagles nest.

(cont)

(cont)

They took the twins,
but stand by me,
brave and unafraid
we will not fear.
They took the twins
but not our spirit,
and together,
tall like towers
we will stand
here in their place.

Cats (a dog perspective)

Lighten up already,
what, with the claws
and the hissing,
somebody step on
your tail this morning?
What's with the licking,
how do you get
your leg pointed
at the ceiling anyway?
Looks like you're
practicing for the ballet.
And that noise you make,
what the heck is
a hair ball anyway?
Just throw up
and be done
with it already.
Don't smirk at me
like that,
at least I go outside,
not in some box
in the corner
for everyone to see.
What do you mean
everyone can see anyway,
hey, I'm just doing
my business over here.

(cont)

(cont)

You don't like it,
don't look.
That's what They do,
pretend there's something
much more interesting
"over there".
So you think
you're so smart,
think you're better
than me, eh?
Well, you bring him
a dead mouse
and I'll fetch his slippers
and let's just see who
gets a cookie first.

Dig (A song?)

We all want love, we search for treasure
The tools we carry dull with age
To dig down deep, time makes it harder
But we keep trying, we chip away

It might be simple, walk the beaches
See what's washed up on the sand
But things that sparkle in the sunshine
Can be worthless in your hand

If you're still searching don't be worried
Get down on your hands and knees
Nothing priceless comes too easy
You just gotta dig to find a diamond

It takes some work, it takes some polish
Time will make that baby shine
It's hard to judge just what you're getting
Until it comes up from the mine

A chunk of rock, a hidden fortune
You wash away the dust and clay
In your hand you hold the brilliance
A rock you almost tossed away

(cont)

(cont)

You've been searching, now you've found it
Down there on your hands and knees
Nothing priceless comes too easy
You just gotta dig to find a diamond

Find a quarter at your feet
Find a dollar in the street
You can pan for gold
In the river wild
But you still gotta dig
To find a diamond

We all want fortune, all want comfort
To sit back for an easy ride
But loves true value we can find it
Just depends how hard we try

Underground, one in a million
A gem that once seemed miles away
Till the shovel hit the surface
Someone found you there today

You've been waiting, now they've found you
Down there on your hands and knees
Nothing priceless comes too easy
You just gotta dig to find a diamond

Wind

The winter wind
knocked lightly,
first trying the door,
and then the shutters,
drawn by the
warm colored lights
that glowed softly
through the windows
framed by the
freshly fallen snow.
A crack in the door jam
was just enough
to let the wind slide
silently through,
to rustle the boughs
of the evergreens
placed neatly around
the old stone hearth.
The gentle laughter
and clink of glasses
beckoned the wind
across the room,
where it paused
only long enough
to brush a lock of hair
out of a little girls eyes
while she lay asleep
upon the couch.

(cont)

The wind sailed softly
through the open doorway.
gently rustling the skirts
and carefully folded napkins
as it moved unseen
around the table.
The playful wind
placed a gentle touch
against a soft cheek
or the nape of a neck,
pushing people closer
and letting them pretend
that it was only
for the warmth.
The wind slowly made
a complete circuit,
listening to all
of the laughter,
and the sighs,
the tales that make up
each single life,
and each family portrait.
A turn here or there
to carry the scent
of the holiday dinner
and to stir the leaves
of the red poinsettia,
then at once

it turned back again
toward the crack
by the door.
The wind brushed
its icy fingers
along the branches
of the brightly lit tree
that stood in the corner,
stirring the ornaments
and colored glass balls.
A short pause,
one last look
over the holiday scene
before it slipped silently
back into the night.
Outside, the wind
puffed its cheeks,
blowing little spirals
in the powdery snow,
and ran its fingers
playfully across
the icicles that hung
from edge of the roof.
Out it went
into the dark,
there were other sights
and other sounds,
more families to visit

(cont)

before the dawn
began to paint
the grey winter sky,
and Christmas morning
came to them all.

Until next time.......................................